LIFE at the RANCH
with OSCAR the Rooster

Gordon Bennett

WestBow Press books may be ordered through booksellers or by contacting:

WestBow Press
A Division of Thomas Nelson & Zondervan
1663 Liberty Drive
Bloomington, IN 47403
www.westbowpress.com
1 (866) 928-1240

Scripture taken from the King James Version of the Bible.

ISBN: 978-1-9736-9736-7 (sc)
ISBN: 978-1-9736-9737-4 (e)

Library of Congress Control Number: 2020913014

Print information available on the last page.

WestBow Press rev. date: 09/16/2020

WESTBOW
P R E S S®
A DIVISION OF THOMAS NELSON
& ZONDERVAN

And God created...every winged fowl after his kind: and God saw that it was good.

Genesis 1:21 (KJV)

DEDICATION

This book about a very special chicken is dedicated to my Dad, Lester Bennett.

When my Dad was growing up in South Dakota, his father always had chickens and even operated a free range chicken farm several miles south of Mitchell, South Dakota, for several years. After my Dad grew up, he began to raise chickens.

When I was growing up in South Dakota and Montana, I watched my Dad really enjoy having chickens around for fresh fryers and eggs. Sometimes in the spring, he would help us hatch several batches of chicks. He continued to have chickens many places where he was a pastor of small churches and through retirement as long as he could.

My Dad taught me all about chickens, chicken houses, chicken coops, roosting areas and nests for eggs. We planned buildings and fences, secured materials, built and rearranged just the right places for chickens. I have been able to have chickens in many places where I have lived and plan to have some more soon.

My dad told a story about his father, my grandfather. When they all lived on a farm near Kennebec, South Dakota, my grandfather decided to build a chicken coop for the chickens that they planned to get. Grampa told his five sons that he would get the material together. Then, the boys could help him build the little building. One Sunday, my grandfather and his sons built the chicken coop in one day. One week later, on Sunday, a tornado went through their farm, picked up only the chicken coop, took it to a neighbor's place, and dropped it! When they found it and inspected it, all that was left of the chicken coop was a pile of kindling! My grandfather made a closing statement, "I guess God didn't want us working on Sunday to build a chicken coop!"

I heard the stories about chickens from my Dad, saw him raise chickens, and helped him many times before having my own chickens. While writing this story about Oscar the rooster, I decided to dedicate it to the memory of my Dad and the ways he taught me how to live through our work with chickens.

Thanks, Dad!
Your son,
Gordon

CREDITS

Special recognition goes to my wife, Norma, for all of her work on my stories. She began by doing all of my typing of term papers and more in college and graduate work. We have worked together on all kinds of projects for years. Now, she works at the computer producing all of the stories that I have written. We have been and are a team. Thank you, Norma!

One day when we were checking on our Arizona ranch, we had to go to pick up some steers. While we were at a small ranchette getting ready to load the steers, a neighbor lady came over to see what was going on. After a little while, she asked us, "Would you like to have a medium size black Bantam rooster?"

Someone asked, "Why do you want to get rid of this rooster?"

The neighbor lady replied, "I have too many roosters, and I need to get rid of this one!"

We answered quickly, "Sure, bring him over, and we will take him with us to Colorado where we have a chicken house with about twenty-five free ranging chickens." We thought that he would fit in there. The neighbor hurriedly went over to her chicken house, caught the black Banty rooster, and brought him to us! What a little sight he was! He weighed about two pounds, was solid black, and had a bright red comb and wattle. His name was Oscar, the Banty rooster!

Soon, we had loaded the steers in the middle space of our stock/horse trailer. Then, we put the rooster in the small space with room for two horses at the front of the trailer. There was a large door between the first space and the middle space. It was solid at the bottom with two open spaces at the top.

Immediately, we left Arizona and traveled to the Colorado ranch. After driving for about an hour, we decided to see how Oscar and the steers were traveling in the trailer. The steers were riding fine, and Oscar was the chief observer. He had jumped or flown up to the open space in the big Door #1 that was between him and the steers. He was perched on the lowest space and was watching all that happened. He seemed very content.

We traveled on and eventually arrived in Colorado that night. When we went to our house, Oscar was still roosting right there on Door #1 in the middle of the lower space. He still seemed very content.

Early the next morning when we went to unload the steers, Oscar was still right there where he had been the night before. We drove down to the barn and unloaded the steers. Then, we went over to the chicken house which was over the hill and down in a little valley from our house and barn. We took Oscar from the trailer and placed him in the chicken house.

After we put Oscar in the chicken house, we stayed around to watch to see how he would get along with the other chickens. There were twenty-five chickens of assorted kinds and sizes. Several Leghorn hens laid white eggs. Several grey and white Barred Rock hens laid brown eggs. Several Rhode Island Red hens laid brown eggs. A few Auracana hens laid blue-green eggs. There was one large Rhode Island Red rooster that we called Big Red. All of these chickens got along well! We hoped that Oscar would get along well with them.

Well, Oscar went straight over to pick a fight with Big Red who was at least twenty inches tall. That did not impress Oscar at all. Although Oscar was only eight inches tall, he obviously was a trained, experienced fighter.

Big Red did not stand a chance. He had never had a fight in his life. He had always been surrounded by hens.

The fight developed quickly, and soon there was blood flying everywhere! Oscar was winning! We jumped into the fight and caught Oscar. We were surprised that Oscar had no physical problems. He was not hurt at all, but Big Red had some bad sores where Oscar had scratched and spurred him. At last, we knew why the lady had been eager to get rid of Oscar. He had a Banty rooster attitude!

As you could guess, Oscar's life went in a new direction. We took Oscar over to the trailer and put him in the front space. We told him that the trailer would be his home at the ranch because we do not like fighting.

After Oscar's fight with Big Red, we fed and watered Oscar in the first space of the trailer. From then on, he roosted every night in his favorite spot right on the middle of the lower space on Door #1. We parked the trailer with its nose toward the northwest to keep Oscar safe when the cold winds would blow.

Oscar soon began his regular trips to Arizona with us when we moved horses. He never made any effort to leave the trailer. It had become his home. He would often get in Space #2 or even Space #3. We soon developed a routine. We would go into the trailer through Door #3 when Oscar was in Space #3. Next, we would open Door #2, and he would go by himself into Space #2. Next, we would open Door #1, and he would go right into Space #1. He knew that Space #1 was his home where he had food and water and shelter from the wind. He seemed to enjoy all the trips to and from Arizona in his secure place. Sometimes, he would make that ten hour trip all by himself. At other times, he would have two to ten horses for company. He did not seem to mind.

Oscar got along with horses better than he did with chickens. We could even put horses in Space #1 and Space #2, and he would always be in his favorite spot, the middle of the lower space on Door #1. He seemed to enjoy a trailer load of horses. Naturally, the trailer would be much warmer on frosty winter days with many horses on board. Between Colorado and Arizona, stopping for fuel became a favorite time for us. As we were refueling, people would see the horses and come over to see them. What a surprise they had when they would see Oscar on his regular perch surrounded by horses. They would laugh and call others to come see the traveling chicken named Oscar with his horse friends.

At other times, people would ask, "What are you hauling?" Our answer was, "Oscar the rooster." Or we would say, "Oscar the rooster with his horses." Most people thought that we were teasing. The story created some fun times. Sometimes, several people gathered around the trailer laughing and talking about Oscar.

One Sunday morning in Colorado, we got up, did our chores, got in the truck and went to church as usual. The small country church, where about 200 of us attended, was about five miles away from our ranch.

After worship was over that special Sunday, we went to our truck to return home. What a surprise awaited us! Beside our truck, scratching in the dirt and gravel was Oscar the rooster. "How did you get here?" we asked.

With some help, we cornered Oscar, caught him and held him while we drove home. After getting home, we discovered that we had left the rear door to the trailer open. Oscar had discovered it, too. He had jumped out, walked near the truck and had jumped up in the motor space to spend the night and had gone with us to church. Some people wondered, "What are you doing with a rooster at church?" We wondered, too.

In looking back, we think that removing Oscar from the chicken house may have saved his life. A few weeks after Oscar's fight with Big Red, we noticed that our flock of chickens was getting smaller in number. We tried to find out why. We looked for animal tracks and chicken feathers. We looked for mountain lions and bobcats. Finally, one morning with about six inches of new snow on the ground, we went to take care of the chickens. As we went around the corner of the chicken house, we surprised a large golden eagle who was carrying away one of our Barred Rock hens which weighed about eight pounds. The eagle must have been close to three feet tall, with a wing span of about six feet. Then, we knew why our chickens were disappearing! After that, we did not have free ranging chickens anymore. We built a covered pen next to the chicken house and locked them all up so the eagles could not get them. If Oscar had not been banned from the chicken house for fighting, he probably would have attacked the eagle and would have lost the fight. However, the eagles never bothered Oscar in his favorite spot in the trailer in the middle of the lower space on Door #1.

We still have many fond memories of Oscar at the ranch. He provided many laughs and entertainment. He was easy to catch and handle. He seemed to enjoy his life in the trailer and all the trips. He surely loved his favorite perch in the middle of the lower space on Door #1. We enjoyed having that little black Banty rooster at the ranch. Maybe you wonder whether Oscar ever stopped fighting. The answer is in the book.

GLOSSARY

Araucana	multi-colored chickens with short legs, known for laying green eggs
Bantam	a very small Breed of chicken. Nickname is Banty.
Barred Rock	gray and white heavy bodied chickens which are raised for meat
Comb	the red ridge on the top of the rooster's head.
Free ranging	usually referring to chickens that are not in a building but are in a yard
Hen	the name of the female chicken that produces eggs and can raise the young chicks after setting on a nest of fertile eggs
Leghorn	white chickens which are usually raised for laying eggs
Rhode Island Red	red heavy bodied chickens which are raised for meat and laying eggs
Rooster	the name of the male chicken that is usually very colorful, with a large comb and wattles, and spurs
Spurs	a naturally occurring pointed growth on the back of male chicken legs that are used for fighting and may be very long and sharp
Steers	male cattle that have been neutered to make them unable to produce young
Wattle	the red hanging down portion on the bottom of the rooster's head.

Look for more of
Gordon Bennett's stories
under the following series:

Dogs of our Lives Series
Grampa's Dog, Shep

BIOGRAPHICAL INFORMATION

Gordon L. Bennett, the author, was born in Glendale, Arizona. Shortly afterward, he moved with his parents to South Dakota where his father helped on the family farm for a couple of years. Then, his father farmed on his own for a couple of years. Later, his father finished his ministry training and volunteered to go to the Bahamas for two years as a Christian missionary. The family returned to South Dakota in time for the author to start school. His father opened a closed church for two years. Next, he started a new church in central South Dakota for three years. It was then that the family moved to the Bitterroot Valley in Western Montana, and the author went to school for grades 6–11. By the time he was in the eleventh grade, he was the oldest of five children.

Much of life there was centered on farm life and church life. The author was involved with all kinds of farm animals and worked for farmers and ranchers in the area. During the summers he did irrigation, put up hay, did tractor work, and helped with building things. Then, the author attended a private high school for his senior year in Kansas. While there, he helped farmers with various kinds of work on Saturdays.

Next, he started his higher education experiences; one year in Kansas, two years in South Carolina where he received his training for church ministry and met and married Norma who is from south Georgia. Then, he spent three years at Willamette University, in Salem, Oregon, for a second B.A. program. Next, he spent six years of graduate work at Western Oregon State University, University of Oklahoma, and Arizona State University. During and after his higher education experiences, he has spent twenty-four years in church ministry and twenty-one years in Academic administration.

For most of his life, the author has enjoyed having a variety of farm animals to care for and to enjoy. Since 2006, the author has been writing true stories about horses, dogs, and other farm animals, all based upon real experiences of life. His favorite dog, so far, was an Australian Shepherd named Sludge. His favorite horse was an AQHA stallion named My Peppy Doc Bar. His favorite pig was a Duroc boar named Big Red. His favorite cow was a Guernsey milk cow named Susie. His favorite sheep was a Romney ewe named Mollie. He wonders which animals will be his next favorites.

Printed in the United States
By Bookmasters